The Last Bucket List

The Last Bucket List

Think Big. Be Changed. Give Life.

David A. Ogren

The Last Bucket List: Think Big. Be Changed. Give Life.

Additional Publications by David A. Ogren

Acoustic Guitar Care 101: A Survival Guide for Beginners

GuitarQuotes: Inspiration from the World's Best Players

Market to Millions: The Ultimate Directory to Free eBook Promotion

TABLE OF CONTENTS

01

SETTING
THE
STAGE

01

"The fear of death follows from the fear of life. A man who lives fully
is prepared to die at any time."

– Mark Twain, American humorist, lecturer

"He gets down to the end of his life, and he looks back and decides
that all those years he suffered, Those were the best years of his life,
'cause they made him who he was. All those years he was happy? You
know, total waste. Didn't learn a thing. So, if you sleep until you're
18… Ah, think of the suffering you're gonna miss. I mean high school?
High school-those are your prime suffering years. You don't get better
suffering than that."

-Frank, Little Miss Sunshine

We each have plans for our lives; hopes and aspirations that may or may not be fulfilled. The interesting thing is that both the events that transpire and the events that don't occur are building blocks to a fulfilling life. We rejoice at success and accomplishments, but also learn from our failures and shortcomings. Sometimes, those defeats can lead to fear, which is a way to insulate ourselves from more failures and hurt. We think that, if we remove the factor of loss, we will be safe and fulfilled. However, what often happens is the creation of an increasingly insular existence as we regularly refuse to risk. A life of closed handedness leads to a type of personal poverty that robs us of community, growth, contentedness and fulfillment.

Perhaps you have heard the old (and varied) tale of the monkey and the jar. The story goes that African hunters would take a piece of fruit, place it in a jar with a small opening, then tie a rope around the top of the jar. After finding an appropriate hiding place, the hunter waits for a monkey to come by and smell the fruit. Upon finding the tasty treat, the monkey reaches inside the jar to take it. After wrapping its fingers around the fruit, the monkey realizes its fist is too large to fit through the jar opening.

The hunter suddenly tugs on the rope, bringing the animal closer and closer. The monkey panics, trying to wrestle the fruit out, but it screeches and scratches to no avail. It must choose to either drop the food and flee to safety or keep the fruit and be captured. Most monkeys are easily trapped because they do not have the foresight to leave short-term gains for long-term life. We often live our lives the same way, being attracted to small "fruits" while abandoning lifelong aims and purposes.

To combat the human tendency of short-sightedness and self-protection, "bucket lists" are often employed as an aid to self-reflection and a tool to determine our ultimate goals. However, many times, these practices end up being nothing more than another means of self-absorption, by simply determining what "I" want to attain, where "I" want to travel, etc. This can lead us back to the narrow confines of our own experiences and desires (do we even know what we want, and can we determine that within ourselves?).

Perhaps it is better to use a bucket list to measure our progress towards becoming the people we want to become. Rather than simply listing all the things we want for ourselves, what if we approached our desires for life from the perspective of pouring life into others? What would that look like? How might we be changed? How would our priorities be altered?

I refer to this as the "life-giving" bucket list: a prioritization of existence that centers on others, bringing vitality and fullness into our lives. As we look beyond our own needs, we gain a greater view of the world around us, simultaneously pouring into others while expanding our own boundaries. Through this orientation, we learn, grow, give and live!

———————————————————————

Here are four primary benefits to a life of giving:

It expands:

A life of giving expands our abilities as we use our talents to help others; it grows our social circles as we interact with different kinds of people; it broadens our ideas about the world around us, how people live, and what impacts others' lives.

It empowers:

Giving enlarges our confidence as we tackle our own fears and perceived deficiencies; it opens new opportunities for education and life learning. However, a life of giving also empowers other people, as we encourage one another and invest in others.

It empties:

A life of giving removes unwanted things, traits, perspectives and desires. When we look beyond ourselves and our own needs, we replace selfishness with generosity, clutter with peaceful space, and closedmindedness with openness.

It enriches:

Lastly, giving enriches our lives. There may be little monetary enrichment, but there will certainly be vigor in activities, community, connections and mindset. A life of giving cultivates our potential, upgrades our abilities and enhances our experiences.

Here are four primary roadblocks to a life of giving:

Selfishness:

As noted, before, selfishness constrains us as we keep things for ourselves. Our attempts to self-protect lead to smallness of thinking, loneliness, and general dissatisfaction with life. The more we isolate ourselves, the less we grow and the less we know.

Small scope:

It is often difficult for us to see beyond our immediate needs and desires and, consequently, we concentrate all our efforts on our ability to define what *we* want in life. This perspective blinds us to others' needs, our true needs, and the potential of both aspirations coming together.

Strain of daily life:

There is no question our lives are busy, and perhaps more fully scheduled than previous generations. Our jobs, credit card debt, electronics and the latest apps can each discourage us from a life of giving. Of course, these things are not bad in themselves, but they can be allowed to take over life "space" until no margin is left to make a full life.

Scarcity of long-range planning:

Like the hunted monkey in the story above, we ignore a life of giving due to our nearsightedness. We don't want to give up the small fruit in exchange for a full life ahead of us but are rather attuned only to the thing(s) in our possession at this moment. This robs us of a tremendous future.

This book attempts to provide a reference point for you to muse, to mull, to meditate. It does not provide answers (each life is too complex for that) but posits questions that will leave you moments to ponder, space to reflect and define concrete steps to learn, grow, give and live!

02

PEOPLE

02

"The people in your life are important. Meaningful relationships with those people are *very* important."

- *Ed Bradley, American Journalist*

"Today we are faced with the preeminent fact that, if civilization is to survive, we must cultivate the science of human relationships—the ability of all peoples, of all kinds, to live together and work together, in the same world, at peace."

- *Franklin D. Roosevelt, in his last public message*

B lair was one of the most successful strategy consultants in his field. Over the past 35 years, he propelled his startup from a ramshackle strip mall office grubbing for short-term contracts, into a top-tier machine, employing 200 hungry operators who aggressively advised, counseled and arm twisted their way into multi-million-dollar contracts. When the money started pouring in, Blair was elated at the thought of paying down his business debts, upgrading his family's lifestyle and even throwing a few bonuses to his zealous staff. As work demands increased, a bit of family time had to be sacrificed. It was necessary, just for a while and only until things were under control, and certainly a small price to pay for the "extras" his family could now enjoy.

However, the joy was soon curtailed, with the mid-90's bringing a few lawsuits against the firm due to some consultations that resulted in bankruptcy for two online startups (one a grocer, and the other a delivery service). The cases tied up the company reserves, and in less than three years, they were close to filing for Chapter 11.

Then, Blair hit on a lead that turned out to be the company's saving grace; a mega-contract with an international bank headquartered in Europe. No more dotcom's and online stores. He would make his hay in the finance industry, and he was even good at it! After word got around that there was a new consultant in investment banking, the dominos fell, bringing in enough work for an army. Blair went about hiring a new platoon of aggressive, arm-twisting advisors who would keep the coffers full and the courts off his back. Now, the days became long and the nights longer, CEO's staggered through the consulting gauntlet, the brown rivers of coffee and whiskey flowed to intensify or temper as needed, and new contracts signed until the Bic pens coughed up the last of their black gel. This was the good life, and there was plenty of it.

The years went at the speed of sound. Blair saw his family less frequently, but made a point of meeting his wife, Karsten, for dinner once a week at least. The annual pilgrimage to their vacation home in Big Sur gave him a chance to catch up with the kids. But, after he delayed the trip one year, his wife and kids started going without him; they didn't seem too bothered. The coughing started on a Tuesday, right after his racquetball game with a new client. When the hacking didn't stop later that night, he went into urgent care. After running all the tests and hearing the words "cancer" and "lungs," he didn't pay much attention to doctor's comprehensive list of treatment plans and approaches. His head hurt more than his lungs right then. Now, Blair was the one being advised and counseled. He wasn't even a smoker. But Blair wasn't a quitter either, and for two years he fought that ugly disease with everything he had, determined to keep his body and his business afloat.

The last two months spent in the special care unit at Redeemer's were painstakingly slow. Things had quieted down quite a bit since turning over the business to the VP. With no work to command his every moment, and space to think, he recalled some of the early years with his ex-wife and kids. They did not have much then, but they had each other, and their Friday nights at Shump's where they downed burgers and fries with the last of their expendable income. Now, Karsten had Martin, the house appraiser, and their quiet abode in the suburbs, away from all the bankers and advisors, the booze and Bic pens.

Blair's nurse came in, adjusting the IV bags and checking the pain med intervals. Who was this one…Audra, Amber? He recalled the kid's unabashed excitement at Christmas, the short, chubby arms jabbing exhausted parents from their slumber before dawn, the rush to tear open gifts, the giggles and squeals, the sweets and coffee. Some things were easily remembered, and others were vague. Was his son's high school baseball team named the Cardinals or the Bluejays? He had missed so many games.

The kids would come by later to say their goodbyes, but first it was Karsten, coming through the door with her "amber waves of grain," Blair's nickname for her perfectly coiffed har.

She sat in the bedside chair, holding Blair's hand in comfortable silence, like two people who had known one other for a long time. There was no judgment or anger. But there was regret. They rested together until the long afternoon sun melted into evening shadows, the weary eyes shutting, the peaks and valleys on the vital signs monitor dropping to an uninterrupted line.

Few of us imagine looking back on a lifetime of experiences and wishing we had spent more time at work. So, why do all the Much of it is due to the "tyranny of the present," which is our propensity to focus on what short-term issues demand our attention. To see what's important, we need to step back from what appears urgent and begin to preemptively define what is truly important. Then, when we're faced with competing interests, we can quickly make a choice that aligns with our previously decided list.

Family and friends are a critical part of experiencing a full life. They create fun, excitement, memories, and, of course, numerous challenges. They can challenge and encourage us, provide support in difficult times, and even hold us accountable and speak into our lives. When you think about people in your life, consider who is currently most important to you, but also who you would like to be in your life, but who may be ostracized in some way through past actions, behaviors or decisions. At the end of your life, who do you want to have shared your life with? What could you do now to avoid future regrets? Here are a few prompts to think through.

1. Roots

What are your roots as a person? Where did you come from? One way to reconnect with the people closest to you is to return to your roots; this could relate to geography, history, people or simply re-evaluating those influences most important to you growing up. Reconnecting authentically with people requires a good idea of who you are as a person, where you came from, and where you are going.

- Along with regaining a connection with your immediate family, do you have a distant relative that you have longed to know?

____

____

____

____

- Have you considered returning to your pre-immigrant homeland to visit your family name "headwaters"?

____

____

____

____

-   Do your children know where you grew up? What would you like to convey to them about your upbringing?

____

____

____

____

-   Have you reviewed your family tree? If not, jot down some relatives that have access to that history, to follow up with later.

____

____

____

____

-   What are the values that your parent(s) passed on to you?

____

____

____

____

-   What values do you want to pass on to your children and friends?

____

____

____

____

2. Reconciliation

To say relationships are difficult and take work is an understatement, and we doubtless encounter challenging personalities in all walks of life. Sometimes, those tests result in fractured ties that last months, years, or even lifetimes. To reconcile means to re-establish, come together, reunite and harmonize. As part of a life-giving bucket list, healing relational bonds should certainly take careful consideration. In some cases, it may be impossible to restore the severed connection, but reconciliation is worth exploring now to avoid regrets in the future.

- Do I have relationships that are broken? List a few of the names.

____

____

____

____

- Do I want to work towards repairing that connection? How do I feel about that?

____

____

____

____

-    What issues or concerns should be considered?

____

____

____

-    What initial steps might I take?

____

____

____

-    Whose help or guidance might I need through this process?

____

____

____

3. Reaching out

Beyond connecting with our own roots and reconciling with broken relationships, there are likely others outside our own circle whose acquaintance would be beneficial (for them and for us!). This approach takes us out of our comfort zone, but also positions us to grow, learn and live. It brings us beyond our own limitations, inviting others into our world that, in turn, brings new opportunities, skills and experiences. Take a chance; step out and reach out.

- I have always wanted to meet…

____

____

____

____

- If we hosted a casual dinner once per month, who would we invite?

____

____

____

____

-   Is there a group or association I have always been interested in?

____

____

____

____

-   Someone who could benefit from my help or expertise would be…

____

____

____

____

-   Who can I identity in my life that needs my help/friendship/expertise?

____

____

____

____

Further Resources

Work/Life balance

- *Off Balance* (Matthew Kelly)
- *Living Forward* (Michael Hyatt)
- *Decide: Work Smarter, Reduce Your Stress, and Lead by Example* (Steve McClatchy)
- *Lead with Balance* (Donnie Hutchinson)

Roots

- *The Everything Guide to Online Genealogy* (Kimberly Powell)
- *Unofficial Guide to Ancestry.com* (Nancy Hendrickson)
- *The Family Virtues Guide* (Linda Kavelin Popov, Dan Popov, John Kavelin)

Reconciliation

- *Healing from Family Rifts* (Mark Sichel)
- *Non-Violent Communication* (Marshall Rosenberg)
- *The Five Languages of Apology* (Gary Chapman)

Reaching Out

- *Daring Greatly* (Brene Brown)
- *Reaching Out* (Henri Nouwen)
- *Playing Tag: You're Not It!* (Glenn Pickering)

03

THINGS

03

We must rapidly begin the shift from a "thing-oriented" society to a "person-oriented" society. When machines and computers, profit motives and property rights are considered more important than people, the giant triplets of racism, materialism, and militarism are incapable of being conquered.

- Martin Luther King, Jr.

"The things you own end up owning you. It's only after you lose everything that you're free to do anything."

- Chuck Palahniuk, Fight Club

2012

was a big year: the "Curiosity Rover" landed on mars, Facebook went public, "#Linsanity" happened, and the Mayan calendar officially ended (glad we dodged that bullet). That year also brought many changes to our family, as we experienced the birth of our third child and prepared to move to Scotland, necessitating a change in employment, housing and budget. As we pondered what to do with all our accumulations over the past seven years, we bandied about the old standards. How about a big garage sale? (lots of work for a few bucks). We could rent a storage unit? (paying to have someone else keep things I don't need).

It was during that time I felt strongly impressed to give away the items we did not plan to take overseas. This was both an exciting and fearful proposition. Perhaps we could help someone else? Do I really want to leave money "on the table" when I have all these moving expenses? After mulling over the options, we decided to take the plunge and really do it. However, we didn't want to simply donate to a place like Good Will, though certainly a fine choice. We hoped to make a personal connection between what we were giving and the people that were receiving.

Through a contact at our church, we found a Cambodian couple working with refugees. These people were coming to Minnesota to start a new life, many arriving with little to no possessions, and were truly starting at the bottom, relying on assistance for things as basic as toothbrushes, soap and non-perishables. The couple came over to our place a few times and we ended up having fun visiting together and loading up our belongings. Since our partial shipping container allotment for Scotland was quite small (150 cubic feet), we needed to give all our large items: couches, armoire, television, queen-size bed, dining room tables, chairs, everything!

A few interesting things resulted from this experience. First, it was incredible knowing that people in such need could make use of the things I didn't need any longer. The personal appreciation and impact seemed to be much greater than simply having a garage sale. Secondly, there was satisfaction in knowing I wasn't just giving my "leftovers," but my very best possessions. The things we gave had value, in the sense that they were still good quality items that were cared for and remained relevant and productive for their purposes. Lastly, there was such joy, freedom and release in the giving. Especially after arriving overseas, I realized I didn't miss any of those things. In fact, life seemed much simpler, less cluttered and more "spaced". All the previous consternation and timidity regarding downsizing and giving things away was completely eclipsed by the truth that consumption and items are not integral to happiness and satisfaction. Those things are often in competition with our highest values.

In 1954, Frederik Pohl wrote a satirical short story on consumerism. Called "The Midas Plague", it centered on the somewhat strange concept of a society so rich, it forces its citizens to consume a quota of goods each day. Great technological breakthroughs have promoted robots to a full, efficient mechanization of all goods, and the world is awash in products. However, this is not a state of Eden. The poorer you are (lower-class), the more consumption is required by the government, while the wealthy have the luxury of smaller quotas. No waste is allowed, and minimum consumption requirements are set which, if not met, drops the citizen down the social ladder, requiring even more consumption.

While we are hard pressed to find a clear correlation between this bizarre society and our own, The Midas Plague has received cult status among its readers as a memorable commentary on humanity's conflicted and sometimes corrupted relationship with "things." Throughout history, we see a shared space in society between humans and the tools and materials they produce, often resulting in a symbiotic ownership (things can "own" us as much as we own the thing). As part of a holistic life assessment, it is appropriate to evaluate our current relationship with consumption and materials to determine if our priorities are in place on our life-giving bucket list. Let's begin by examining our attitude toward "things."

1. Attitude

We commonly have a "love/hate" relationship with things since items provide benefits to its owners, as well as require something. The acquisition of belongings may bring certain conveniences and comfort, but it also provides more items to maintain, insure, upgrade, back-up, replace and worry about. Now, as things become more animated and interactive, it appears things could have a relationship with us, owning and managing our time for us as we become increasingly dependent. As with many ingrained patterns, our feelings and assumptions about consumerism and buying things comes from a wide range of influences, including family, income, social context, values, etc. Here are a few things to ponder:

- Growing up, how were consumer items viewed in my home?

____

____

____

____

- How do I currently feel about the number of my belongings? (excited, stressed, encouraged, burdened?)

____

____

____

____

-   Am I more overwhelmed or satisfied by the "things" in my life?

____

____

____

____

-   How might my emotions, self-perception and confidence be linked to things I own?

____

____

____

____

-   To what degree might purchasing things affect my mood, hopes and aspirations?

____

____

____

____

2. Analyze

Often, we have difficulty stepping back to notice how products, technology and consumerism have shaped our lives. Social patterns and norms become so ingrained that we take them for granted. Since marketing techniques and data are becoming so pervasive, ads are customizable on our browsers, email applications and online store accounts based on recent shopping and search activity.

The growing connectedness and the "internet of things" will only increase the data available, marketing and product range, making it extremely difficult to remove one's heart and mind from products' claims on our time and attention. Of course, numerous positive developments can (and have) resulted from all these developments. However, our exercise here is to momentarily slow down and assess. Let's stop and take a moment to consider our current relationship with "things."

- What owned items require most of my time?

____

____

____

____

____

- Does the time spent with those items correlate to the items' worth?

____

____

____

____

- Are certain items robbing me of what is more highly prioritized?

____

____

____

____

- What adjustments might I want to make in my consumption?

____

____

____

____

-   How do I currently define "want" and "need," and do the ads
    targeted to us define those terms the same way?

____

____

____

____

3. Articulate and Reprioritize

A correct understanding and use of "things" in our lives does not necessarily mean a simple purge. As you ponder the questions below, note the items you can do without or give away to benefit others, but also note the things you can achieve with those things out of the way. Perhaps there are some goals or other items that would really benefit you now that you've made room for them! For instance, perhaps someone always wanted to learn to sail but was distracted by weekends of TV watching, video gaming, or shopping. If that person prioritized sailing, what would that look like in this context? What could be re-prioritized to allow more time, resources and energy to be placed into a life-giving experience? This is our time to spell out our next steps - to "award" (gift) to others - but also to settle what is truly important in our hearts and make room for that.

- What items would I be best served without (what is compromising my highest priorities)?

____

____

____

____

-    What room in my house causes me the most stress?

____

____

____

____

-    What person(s) in my life would benefit from some of my things?

____

____

____

____

-    With that item(s) gone, what dream/passion can I now focus on?

____

____

____

____

-   With fewer things, what new resources would I have at my
    disposal?

____

____

____

____

Further Resources

Attitude towards "stuff"
- *The Story of Stuff* (Annie Leonard)
- *The Paradox of Choice* (Barry Schwartz)
- *The Overspent American* (Juliet B. Schor)

Analyze our "stuff"
- *Making Peace with the Things in Your Life* (Cindy Glovinsky)
- *Clutter Busting* (Brooks Palmer)
- It's All Too Much (Peter Walsh)

Articulate and Reprioritize "stuff"
- *The Joy of Less* (Francine Jay)
- *Organizing from the Inside Out* (Julie Morgenstern)
- *The Life-Changing Magic of Tidying Up* (Marie Kondo)

04

CAREER

04

"The future cannot be predicted, but futures can be invented."

- Dennis Gabor, Nobel Prize Winner 1971

"At every stage of my career, I sought out the most influential people around me and asked for their help and guidance."

- Keith Ferrazzi, Ferrazzi Greenlight

"What do you do for a living?"

Aubrey's eyes darted around the reception room, a dreary veteran's hall filled with sagging balloons, dry ham sandwiches, a few relatives and mostly strangers. She had regretted agreeing to come to her Aunt's retirement party. That was two hours ago. Now, she was searching for the nearest exit so she could get out of those terrible shoes, the stifling atmosphere, and monotonous small talk. Why was the music so loud? The most recent inquisition came from a debonair man in his '70s, dark trimmed mustache, and tailored suit making him look like an extra on the set of "The Philadelphia Story". Aubrey imagined him to be a successful CEO or banker, or something that makes people independently wealthy - a position far removed from her own life.

Now, the sandwich bite was halfway down, the shoes were most uncomfortable, and she had to fumble for an answer, trying to think of an ingenious way to describe her dog-washing business as a society-transforming non-profit. She was doing her best to impress, but her words sounded more like Elaine from Seinfeld eating Jujy Fruits. "I run a high-end pet maintenanthe enterprithe that theeks to improve the quality of life for all partithipanths."

"Pardon, could you repeat that?," inquired the polite, debonair man.

Aubrey winced at the inevitable round two of communication. She chewed as fast as possible, willing the dry food down. It wasn't enough. "I run a high…I wath dogs right now…uh, for people."

Debonoir Man looked quizzical, now leaning closer to hear, close enough to smell ham sandwiches. "Ah, you clean things for people…" He seemed befuddled but also relieved to have finally mastered this word jumble.

Aubrey could not muster enough energy for round three. It was time to make quick work of this conference on her career path and escape to better environments. With one last manic chew, the final sandwich piece beginning its slow descent, she stood to her full stature of five feet, forced a smile and bellowed over the music.

I WASH DOGS FOR RICH PEOPLE!

The song blasting over the speakers halted abruptly as Aubrey hollered "WASH," leaving the hall with an empty audio palette, except for her now irretrievably boisterous description, resounding against the back wall, now booming back as some strange social critique. "Rich people…rich people…dogs."

Ten or fifteen heads turned her way, searching for the source of this disruptive cry.

Debonair Man snapped straight up and wrinkled his nose, as if preparing to salute and avoid bad odors simultaneously. He appeared paler now, taking out a handkerchief and looking frantically for a place to sit. With no chairs nearby, he glanced back at Aubrey. "Quite right, quite right," he faltered, "that's very….," before shuffling off toward the sandwich table.

The thing was, Aubrey loved dogs, had a thriving business of repeat customers, had plenty to live on, and enough time to do other things. Why does it matter what I do, Aubrey thought, and why do I feel uncomfortable talking about it?

———————————————————

1. Career Discovery

Finding our place in the world involves many things; among them are identifying passions, gifts, abilities and preferences. This journey is often filled with detours, wrong turns, and a few decisions that are spot on. However, each of these experiences feeds into the process of discovery, as we would be unable to avoid our dislikes without first defining what works and what does not work. Our careers hold a prominent place in our lives because they demand much of our time and form much of our identity (for better or worse).

Part of the "life-giving bucket list" career approach is to honestly evaluate our current state of work. As you work through the questions below, consider your immediate place of work, your education history (formal or informal), your gifts, and how those agree together. Often, tension comes from living a life of dissonance between ourselves and our work.

-   How would I describe my satisfaction with my current work?

____

____

____

____

____

-   To what degree does my work line up with my education?

____

____

____

-   To what degree does my work link up with my abilities?

____

____

____

-   To what degree does my work line up with my passion?

____

____

____

- What is more important to me: doing what I am most passionate about, or working where I am most effective (fulfillment vs. impact)?

____

____

____

____

2. Career Expansion

If you find you are unhappy with your current career, a change may not provide the positive outcome you are looking for. Sometimes, the answer is right in front of you, available within your current company, co-workers and role. Rather than approaching our work frustrations with a victim mentality (this is happening to me), let's look for places to impact and change (I am "happening" to this company).

Remember, you have something to offer your manager, co-workers and context that no one else can - you! You have skills, experiences and abilities that are not represented unless you are truly "there" 100%. As Gandhi famously said, "Be the change you want to see." Look for a problem you can solve this week. Identify resources you need, then ask for them. The worst that can happen is your manager knows you are thinking independently and creatively. You don't have to change careers to grow your life now.

- What skills could I improve upon in my current work?

-   How can I expand my influence right where I am?

____

____

____

-   What resources do I need to improve those skills?

____

____

____

-   What people might assist me in this growth?

____

____

____

- Who should I talk to next week about this (who is able to empower me now)?

____

____

____

____

3. Career transition

Perhaps you can find no agreement with your current manager, company vision, or revised job description. Maybe you just feel burnt out. One of the most important things to remember is that it is never too late. Life is too short for regrets. Don't wait for "sometime" or "when things settle down." Things will never settle down. If you believe you are at the threshold of a new career season, talk with people you trust, whether life mentors, friends or family. Vocalize your frustrations (motives are important in discerning career changes), your ideas (brainstorming can clarify things in your own mind) and your plan of action (ambiguous proposals lead to indefinite results).

As you work through that process, your potential career transition will become more fully formed. Haste is rarely beneficial with these types of decisions, so make sure you get all the information you need, get feedback from those you trust, and gain input from those already in the new career.

-   What have I always wanted to do, but never pursued?

____

____

____

____

____

-

\-   What unique skills could I bring to that new work?

____

____

____

____

\-   What opportunities have I ruled out before trying?

____

____

____

____

\-   How can I replace "it's too late" with "it's possible now"?

____

____

____

____

-   Who can help me with this transition?

Further Resources

Career Discovery

- *The Art of Work* (Jeff Goins)
- *Do What You Are* (Paul D. Tieger)
- *Designing Your Life* (Bill Burnett)
- *The Pathfinder* (Nicholas Lore)

Career Expansion

- *So Good They Can't Ignore You* (Cal Newport)
- *Do Over* (Jon Acuff)
- *The Success Principles* (Jack Canfield)

Career transition

- *What Color is Your Parachute* (Richard N. Bolles)
- *Second-Act Careers* (Nancy Collamer)
- *The Joy of Not Working* (Ernie J. Zelinski)

05

FINANCES

05

The greatest wealth is a poverty of desires.

– Seneca

Try not to become a man of success, but rather try to become a man of value.

- Albert Einstein

Paul Davis was CEO of a large semi-conductor manufacturer in Austin, striving to push his company into the Fortune 500. After running through decades and countless 80-hour weeks, the board demanded Paul take a two-month sabbatical "refocus" and "refresh." Paul felt like they were inferring he "remove" and "retire." "What if they've moved on by the time I return?," he thought. But there was no dissuading the board, so the following Saturday he planted himself in his first-class seat, flying to Ibiza, Spain to take in the Mediterranean sun and air. "What will I do on an island for two months?"

Paul loved the island, then hated it, then loved it again. It was culture shock at an advanced rate.

Paul quickly found his favorite restaurants, beaches and golf spots.

One day, he strolled past town, into the countryside. Taking in the warm sun, he felt he could walk for hours. About one mile out of Ibiza, he noticed a small dirt road disappearing over a grassy hill. Taking the detour, he was surprised to find a beautiful olive grove on the other side. The main house, outbuildings and grounds were meticulous, and the combined smells of olives, soil and grass brought a relaxed frame of mind that Paul forgot existed.

The owner, Miguel Cardona, was happy to give a tour, including the olive harvesting, pressing, preparing, packaging and shipping. "This is incredibly impressive!," Paul exclaimed as they feasted over fresh bread, olive oil, tomatoes, salami and wine. The wheels were turning, and Paul was already considering helping Miguel with his business. He just needed some details: profit margins, competition, distribution.

Are you selling internationally, he wanted to know. No, Miguel had not considered that. What about expanding the fields? No, Miguel could not afford more land. Paul asked, "Well, how many hours per day do you work?" Miguel thought for a few minutes. "I work when I need to. Some weeks are busy, such as harvest time. Other weeks, we just do some maintenance." "Well, what do you do the rest of the time?," Paul inquired. Miguel smiled, "I strum my guitar, play with my children and sip wine on the porch at sunset. Paul was growing exasperated. "Miguel, let me help you expand this business. I know exactly what to do. You could be doubling your profits by next year!"

"What would I do with all the extra money?," Miguel wanted to know.

"You could start selling in mainland Europe, then on to North America. We'll set up an international office in a city like Madrid or Barcelona to manage everything. The sky's the limit. People will love this olive oil!," proclaimed Paul.

"Ok, but what would I do after selling my product in so many countries?"

Paul responded immediately, "We'll go public and sell stock, then you'll have more capital to invest in retail shops, online marketing and more olive groves in more countries! We'll come full circle from raw to finished products."

Miguel was pensive, brow furrowed, deep in thought. "Ok, but what comes after that?".

"Well, you retire a wealthy man, of course. Then, you can move to a beautiful quiet place, relax and enjoy all the things of life!," Paul shouted.

"I could enjoy things like playing with my family, strumming my guitar and sipping wine on the porch at sunset?," Miguel ventured.

Paul sat in the chair, visually stunned, hand still raised in the air from his last point. The wheels in his mind were no longer spinning, having abruptly halted at the olive farmer's last response. His raised hand came down as they observed the olive groves and the last rays of the day's sun. He had much to consider - not about the olive groves, but about his own life. After sitting in silence for a few minutes... "Miguel, can I ask you one more question?" Miguel looked both expectant and worried. "Could I have more bread and olives?," Paul asked.

"Yes, of course! There is always more," Miguel joyfully replied.

Miguel's wife and two children joined them on the porch. "I'll get my guitar as well", Miguel said, as he disappeared into the house.

1. Our Attitudes towards Money

Our perceptions about the fundamental aspects of money often go unarticulated in our lives. This is for good reason, as it is easy to take something so ubiquitous for granted. We move through our day, responding to impulses and acting on desires, but rarely do we delve into the foundational influences upon our relationship with cash. Taking care of business, we buy what we need or want, we pay the bills, and we might save a little. Observing those around us, we quickly label each other as savers or spenders, deliberate or spontaneous.

However, we need to define the root cause of our behavior, understanding ourselves and our environment before effectively harnessing money's influence. It is helpful to understand the forces, relationships and attitudes that have brought us this far before looking at basic financial planning, investing and retirement. Let's use the questions below to start the process:

- Growing up, how was money perceived/used in my family? (e.g., openly discussed; privately held)

____

____

____

____

-   What attitudes towards money have I carried into adulthood?

____

____

____

____

-   What motivates my current use of money? (fear, status, charity, desires, needs, security)

____

____

____

____

-   How would I describe contentment, and would I describe myself as content?

____

____

____

____

-   Is money a "driver" of behavior or a "tool" I use? (am I controlled by it or do I control it?)

____

____

____

____

2. Beginning Financial Planning

Trying to get your financial "house" in order can be quite intimidating at the beginning, especially if your current budget is to stop buying things once your checking account is depleted. Fear not! The path to improvement is a life-long process and involves daily decisions. You don't have to fix everything today, but you can start with something. The most important decision you can make now is to begin the journey, being transparent about your current situation and gathering resources and mentors to assist you.

Secondly, you are not alone. Almost everyone encounters financial challenges, but many do not face them squarely or ask for help. The questions and resources below will empower you towards steps of financial freedom. Whether you are at the beginning of the journey, or things are well in hand, you will find something to challenge and push you forward as you assess, refocus and re-prioritize. You can do this!

- What type of budget do I have, and am I following it?

____

____

____

____

- How much debt do I currently have?

____

____

____

____

- Have I sat down with a financial planner to assess my current financial picture?

____

____

____

____

- Do I have any financial "gaps"? (lacking insurance, no savings, late fee charges)

____

____

____

____

-   What are my financial priorities for the next year? Five years?

____

____

____

-   Are my spouse and I on the same page with our financial priorities?

____

____

____

-   What is something I can do next week to improve my financial picture?

____

____

____

3. Investing

Growing your savings is not just for that wealthy uncle of yours that you haven't heard from in fifteen years (but hope to hear from soon). The worst type of investing is waiting for something good to fall into your lap. Expanding your capital takes planning, knowledge and real work. The second worst type of investing is waiting until you have more money to begin contributing to that mutual fund, etc. The earlier you start, the better. If you are a teenager, or just entering the workforce, I encourage you to plan your budget (under the guidance of a professional) around your long-term investment. If you are forty or fifty years old, don't give up just because you only have fifteen to twenty-five years of work left. Find a wise investment you can add to every month. Give whatever you can. Even small beginnings can become major gains under the law of compounding interest.

- Am I aware of basic investing principles? How would I describe those principles?

____

____

____

____

- Does/did my family contribute to investment funds? If so, how did that take place (monthly, direct withdrawal, lump sum)?

____

____

____

____

- Have I determined a consistent, monthly amount to set aside? What might that look like?

____

____

____

____

- Which investing formats might be best for me? (Roth IRA, 401K, Mutual Funds, ETFs, etc.)

____

____

____

____

- How can I maximize my contributions through offerings at work, personal funds, etc.?

____

____

____

____

- Which professional could I contact to assess my situation?

____

____

____

____

4. Retirement

Money and retirement: the two often influence each other in ways we do not anticipate until it is too late. Some people wanted to retire early, but never looked at the practical sacrifices necessary to meet their goals. Others find themselves working (at least part-time) until later in life due to lack of planning. Still others pass away before laying out the plan of estate disbursement to their loved ones, leaving behind additional legal costs and turmoil. The good news is that you and I can begin to plan for our retirement and our families' care right now. Let's not wait until we are close to 65 years old before anticipating our future needs. Laying the groundwork now takes foresight, discipline and professionally informed people to guide us along the way - but it is worth the effort. The decisions we make today will affect the future for ourselves and our families. So, let's get started!

- When do I want to retire?

____

____

____

____

____

- How much money will I need to retire at that age? (online calculators can be helpful)

____

____

____

____

- Do I need to adjust my expectations? If so, how?

____

____

____

____

- What will I use my money for during retirement? (besides necessities)

____

____

____

____

- Will I need to live somewhere else? (reduce expenses)

____

____

____

- Do I have an estate plan? If not, when will I start one?

____

____

____

- Which professional should I contact to assess my current state and plan for the future?

____

____

____

5. Giving

Saving and budgeting are extremely important aspects of a robust fiscal picture. However, giving financially is also a major building block to a healthy life. Giving is an active reminder that we need each other, that there are always people in need, and that we do not live simply to stockpile cash. Giving also connects us with other people, organizations and opportunities, where we can really make a difference in someone else's life. Think of the times that you have been on the receiving end of someone else's unselfishness. It can be a life-altering occasion! Let's take a moment to remind ourselves that gratitude, thankfulness and generosity can go hand-in-hand, enriching our experiences and bringing our lives into the orbit of others. Just as we have been helped, we can also give strategically and purposefully to assist others in need and pass on the blessing.

- What does my current giving look like (charitable organizations, non-profits, etc.)?

____

____

____

____

____

- Am I comfortable with my giving goals, or do they need to be revised?

____

____

____

____

- Does my current giving line up with my priorities, passions and values?

____

____

____

____

- How does my budget represent those ideals and values?

____

____

____

____

Further Resources

Our Attitudes towards Money
- *The Soul of Money* (Lynn Twist)
- *Happy Money: The Sciences of Happier Spending* (Elizabeth Dunn, Michael Norton)
- *Money, Possessions and Eternity* (Randy Alcorn)
- *Love Your Life, Not Theirs* (Rachel Cruze)

Beginning Financial Planning
- *Get a Financial Life: Personal Finance in Your Twenties and Thirties* (Beth Kobliner)
- *The Total Money Makeover* (Dave Ramsey)
- *The Total Money Makeover Workbook* (Dave Ramsey)
- *The Millionaire Next Door* (Thomas J. Stanley)
- *The One-Page Financial Plan* (Carl Richards)

Investing
- *A Beginner's Guide to Investing* (Alex Frey, Ivy Bytes)
- *The Little Book of Common Sense Investing* (John Bogle)
- *The Intelligent Investor* (Benjamin Graham)
- *The Only Investment Guide You'll Ever Need* (Andrew Tobias)

Retirement
- *Retirement Planning in 8 Easy Steps* (Joel Kranc)
- *How to Make your Money Last* (Jane Bryant Quinn)
- *Can I Retire Yet?* (Darrow Kirkpatrick)
- *How to Retire Happy, Wild, and Free* (Ernie J. Zelinski)

Giving

- *Give Smart* (Thomas J. Tierney)
- *Inspired Philanthropy* (Tracy Gary, Kim Klein)
- *Giving 2.0* (Laura Arrillaga-Andreesen)
- *Money Well Spent* (Paul Brest)

06
LIVE &
LOCAL
06

There is no power for change greater than a community discovering what it cares about.

- Margaret J. Wheatley, management consultant

The greatness of a community is most accurately measured by the compassionate actions of its members.

- Coretta Scott King

Jacinta was down on her luck. More than that, she was down on herself. After moving from the familiar sun of Arizona to a promising job in Chicago in October, Jacinta worked harder than ever to establish herself in the unfamiliar work, social circles and expectations of her new environment at La Rabida Children's Hospital. She made it through Thanksgiving (two calls to mom in Tucson, one to her sister in Dallas), but Christmas proved to be too much, precipitating an unplanned red-eye flight home for a few days. After reconnecting with family and friends, it took a panicked call from Ronnie, the scheduling lead on her floor, reminding Jacinta of the shift on Tuesday, that prompted the begrudging trip back to Tucson International for the flight back.

The new year fed into February, then March, continuing the long, blustery winter. Jacinta fell into a rut of loneliness, busyness and detachment. Now it was early April, and her birthday was five days away, on the eleventh. "What's wrong with me?," she questioned as she wrapped up another crazy weekend shift, eager to get back to the apartment and order some deep-dish delivery. She loved her career and coworkers at La Rabida but felt disconnected and weary. Jacinta recalled her activity and engagement with the local Tucson community, and missed the neighbors and friends who would converge on their Eastside home for block parties, summer cookouts and birthdays. "Even birthdays," she thought. "But here I am, all alone in this city."

Then, Jacinta had the most peculiar, audacious idea. What if all the lonely people with April birthdays came together to celebrate? "Then, I would meet all kinds of people and we would start off with one thing in common," she ventured. But, how does one find strangers with April birthdays, then invite them for a party? Craigslist was too creepy, Facebook did not reveal enough Chicago contacts, and email was a no-go. Jacinta thought about the neighborhood newspaper, "The Bloc". She could list a classified ad, inviting people to come to a party in the community room on the first floor of her apartment building. Now, she was excited, thinking about making five new friends before the end of April 11. Jacinta dialed the number for "The Bloc", was quickly transferred to the classifieds department, and read from her prepared ad.

The paper took her information, promising that the ad would go out the next day, for four consecutive days. Jacinta then ordered a large sheet cake from Marco's to be delivered on the eleventh, and checked her stock of coffee, Pepsi and lemonade. "What if nobody comes," she speculated, "This is kind of strange after all." The following days flew by with busy shifts at La Rabida and finishing up plans for the party. Even some of her coworkers noticed the ad. "Is that your invitation Jacinta?," and "I've never thought of doing that before," she would hear. That's a nice way of saying "What in the world are you doing?," Jacinta thought. On the afternoon of the eleventh, after work Jacinta set up tables in the common room, brought board games down from her apartment and got the food and drinks set out. As 7pm approached, her nerves set in, causing her to rethink the plan. "This was a bad idea. No one is here, and I am going to look like a fool, standing in the empty room of my own party."

At 7:05, an elderly couple came in the room. Jacinta, thrilled, shouted "Happy birthday, so glad you could come!" "I'm Marion," the grandmother said firmly, adding "this doesn't look like bingo..."
"Oh, I think bingo is in the smaller room at the end of the hall."

"Not going that far," said Marion stubbornly, "what's going on here?"

"Well, I'm having a party for people with April birthdays," Jacinta stated, now a bit deflated.

"Looks like a humdinger," Marion intoned. "Albert," she hollered at her husband, "we're staying here for the party; make yourself comfortable." Albert did as he was told, and Marion sauntered over to the cake table. Jacinta sighed, ready to excuse herself to go back to the apartment.

Then, a family with young children, two boys, entered the room. "Hi, is this the April Partyers Club?," the father asked expectantly, "my wife's birthday is today, and we just moved here." Soon following were a U of Chicago economics major named Marni, a couple from Eritrea, and two singles from Jacinta's apartment building. Now, the common room was bubbling with conversation, food and fun. Games were set up, presents were loaded on the table near the door, and cake was passed around. More arrived after 8pm, including a sales director named Paul and two brothers from India, Vihaan and Kabir, studying engineering. The night was a complete success, with stories told, laughs (and some tears) shared, and new friendships kindled, ending with the promise to keep in touch and meet again next year.

Before leaving, Marion invited everyone to her son's place on Lake Michigan for some boating in May. "Now Albert, you remind me," she commanded as Albert tried his best to save the date on his new phone. After all was cleaned up and everyone had gone home, Jacinta was back in her apartment, grateful for her new friends, feeling energized and connected again. "My problem was," she reflected, "I just needed to belong again."

We can easily view investing into our community as too great of a commitment, or beyond our abilities and giftings. However, being "live and local" and present in our neighborhoods, workplaces, schools and communities often means simply seeing a need and reaching out in the best, human way possible.

Jacinta took a need (even a loss) and turned it from an inward, narcissistic perspective, to an outward invitation to "others." This brought an opportunity for empowerment, connectedness, and belonging. The profound truth is that community outreach can be seen in small attitudes or large projects. You can find your place by looking beyond yourself to the needs of others. Before doing that, it helps to understand your local context and needs.

1. Discovering the Context

The first step to investing in our local communities is to understand our town, neighborhood, and the people within them. Some are vibrant bastions of life, assistance and growth, while others are decaying blocks of poverty, isolation and decline. Most of our communities are likely somewhere in between; an average mix of possibilities, frustrations and casual recognition. But we need to get beyond the ignoring and avoidance. Let's identify potential gaps or problem areas in our neighborhoods before we consider ways we can use our abilities and ideas to encourage positive change. A good place to start is to understand our own experience of loneliness and belonging. The emotions of humanity are common to us all; if you have felt a certain way before, many other have as well. The questions below will help to "get the ball rolling."

- What do I feel is missing in my neighborhood/community?

____

____

____

____

____

-   How would I describe the relationship between my neighbors?

____

____

____

____

-   Have I struggled with loneliness before? If so, what effect did it have on me?

____

____

____

____

-   How might a determined involvement in my community aid a sense of belonging/purpose?

____

____

____

____

2. Encouragement and Perspective

Amid the barrage of negative news and isolated busyness, we can easily become discouraged and withdrawn. However, many positive things occur around us each day. Do we observe and notice them, or do we allow them to pass us by as we are monopolized by the tyranny of the urgent? There is a big difference between the "urgent" and the "important." The important things are often those attitudes we want to encourage regularly; like solidarity, respectfulness, responsibility, ownership etc. We can be encouraged as we underscore our values and highlight those people and actions that lead to the change we seek. There is a meaningful correlation between the things we think about, the things we tell ourselves, and our resulting actions and behaviors. Let's take a few moments to identity important things we can be thankful for, people we can commend and impressions we can affirm.

-   What positive things are happening in my town right now?

____

____

____

____

____

-   Who can I encourage in their work? (write, call, invite for coffee?)

____

____

____

____

-   What positive experiences with groups have I had in the past?

____

____

____

____

-   Who would I describe as an impactful citizen?

____

____

____

____

3. Practical Community Outreach

Lastly, let's practically look at what we can offer to those around us. It's easy to be overwhelmed by the need or to discount our ability to make a difference. However, even small acts of kindness can change relationships and build things for the future. Remember, it's ok if the problem you see is not a "big" governmental issue. Start small but start with something and make it "personal." For example, does your neighborhood have a "welcoming committee" for new neighbors. If you are a mechanic, plumber, home builder, etc., how can you use that skill to help others nearby? Also, use the great benefit of networking in community outreach. You don't have to figure this out all alone. Talk to someone who has done this before and is currently involved in the community. How did they find their place? Community outreach should essentially be practical, putting "feet" to our ideas and getting out there.

-   What are my passions/gifting at this stage of my life?

____

____

____

____

____

-    How can I use that passion to assist others in my community?

____

____

____

-    Who can I contact to learn more about current local needs?

____

____

____

-    What is the first small step I can make to impact those around me?

____

____

____

Further Resources

Discovering the Context

- *Bowling Alone* (Robert D. Putnam)
- *The Art of Community* (Charles Vogl)
- *Tribe* (Sebastian Junger)
- *Community: The Structure of Belonging* (Peter Block)

Encouragement and Perspective:

- *Your Next 24 Hours: One Day of Kindness Can Change Everything* (Hal Donaldson)
- *In the Neighborhood* (Peter Lovenheim)
- *Population: 485 - Meeting Your Neighbors One Siren at a Time* (Michael Perry)
- *Soul of a Citizen* (Paul Rogat Loeb)
- *Let Your Life Speak* (Parker J. Palmer)

Practical Community Outreach

- *Make a Difference: America's Guide to Volunteering and Community Service* (Arthur I. Blaustein)
- *How to be an Everyday Philanthropist* (Nicole Bouchard Boles)
- *Doing Good Better* (William MacAskill)
- *Introduction to Community Development* (Jerry W. Robinson, Gary Paul Green)

07

TRAVEL

07

Travel is fatal to prejudice, bigotry, and narrow-mindedness, and many of our people need it sorely on these accounts. Broad, wholesome, charitable views of men and things cannot be acquired by vegetating in one little corner of the earth all one's lifetime.

- Mark Twain, American humorist, lecturer

The real voyage of discovery consists not in seeking new landscapes, but in having new eyes.

- Marcel Proust, French novelist

"The gold package comes with two jet skis and includes a bottle of champagne," Doug pointed out hopefully, brow raised, followed by "the silver only includes the champagne…" He and his wife Sonja had been pouring over high-gloss travel brochures for about two hours, and the numbness was beginning to set in. Sonja took another big gulp of green tea. "Yes," she responded, "but we could take the money we save from the jet skis and do that snorkeling outing instead." "I don't snorkel anymore," Doug retorted. "Remember my bad experience in Barbados?" Sonja suppressed an eye roll. "If he had just followed the class instructions, instead of going off by himself to that reef," she thought.

This current planned trip to Tahiti, initially a spontaneous notion, was quickly becoming laborious. Sonja wanted to save money and go "off the beaten path," while Doug wanted to go all out, making their time memorable. Sonja wanted to explore local restaurants, while Doug thought it made sense to spring for the all-inclusive meals at the resort. With so many options, packages, stars and tiers, it was hard to tell if they were getting closer to a decision or approaching a meltdown. All this relaxing was getting stressful.

Every year, they travelled somewhere. Four years ago, it was cruising on the Caribbean, funded by a Groupon they stumbled upon late in January. They trotted from island to island in that giant white ship, enjoying the sun deck, endless buffets, and shopping at seaport markets. The evening lineups were filled with concerts, shows and late happy hours where they sampled gourmet cocktails in swanky clubs. The following year, it was the timeshare in Goa, India that Doug's uncle Preston rented out to them for ten days. It was time to cash in their airmiles anyway, so why not? They sampled the prawns and samosas but avoided the Kalputi (fish head curry). With endless beaches at hand, Doug and Sonja made a point of taking a sunset stroll each night.

Last year, Sonja's work sent her to Barcelona, Spain to assist with some accounting at their international office. She and Doug decided to extend her stay so they could catch some rays along the Mediterranean and savor the regional wines and seafood. None of these trips were terribly expensive. Coupons, travel perks, work reimbursements and savings all helped to make it possible. They had always been careful with their spending habits, and, after all, deserved to get away from their hectic schedules once a year.

It was relaxing to escape, and exciting to visit new places. However, the resorts, timeshares and cruises, the white tablecloths, tennis courts and afternoon drinks, the prompt service, well-manicured lawns and compound walls were all beginning to blend together into an in-discernable stream of sunshine, seafood, formal dinners and white sandy beaches. Just last year, they caught themselves before accidentally booking the same hotel again, aptly named "Double Palms Resort". Now, as plans for this years' trip became a battle of wills tempered with exhaustion, a nagging concern began to emerge.

Doug shoved the brochures aside, ready to give up and book another trip to the Double Palms. It was either that, or go see the in-laws in Tampa, which was a cheap, but not particularly enticing alternative. He wouldn't offer that idea unless Sonja brought it up. "Please don't bring it up," Doug thought. He folded his arms and let out a sigh, a bit too vociferously, when Sonja spoke what he was already thinking. "I feel like we've done this trip a million times before. I want a different way to see and experience things. There must be a different way to do this." Doug looked at the kitchen table, piled with ads and brochures from their travel agent. They all seemed to have the same pictures of palm trees, beaches and food. "A different way to travel?," Doug wondered aloud.

Then, they started reminiscing about their college days, when they had ideas and ideals; back when they felt they could do something special with their lives. Sonja had spent time in the Peace Corp, and Doug had taught English in Chile for a summer. That seemed like a lifetime ago. What about now? Could they make a difference in someone's life? Could they make a difference in the world? "I have an idea," Sonja ventured. "It doesn't include champagne, but it will be memorable." Doug's eyes lit up.

----

1. A Broader Definition of Travel

When it comes to bucket lists, travel is always a hot topic. A quick review of the ads in your local newspaper, online websites, or the travel section at your bookstore will convince you that going to new lands is consistently alluring (and big business!). We easily dream of all the beautiful, exotic places we could explore around, relax in, and travel through. However, historically, travel has been about much more than heading off to the new, chic destination. Excursions and touring also invite us to new experiences, open doors of culture and help us learn about ourselves. There is not one correct way to travel, and the purposes and options are endless! Let's think about our own understanding of travel.

- Initially, what inspires your desire to travel? (new experiences, learning, scope, etc.)

____

____

____

____

____

-   What might discourage your plans to travel? (finances, logistics, unfamiliar circumstances, etc.)

____

____

____

____

-   How would you measure the value of excursions? (to be challenged, entertained, stimulated, etc.?)

____

____

____

____

-   How might you redefine travelling, globe-trotting, or adventure now, in comparison to a previous age?

____

____

____

____

2. Memorable Stories

When we think about travel, what inspires us? Are they classic tales of exploration and mapping, or the colorful tales you hear from your uncle during the holidays? Stories both underscore our shared values and challenge us to meet our ideals. Take a moment to share some of your favorite travelling stories with someone special. You may find examples of pure traveling bliss, while others will relive some "can you believe that happened?" moment, or a pledge that "I'm never doing that again!" Whatever the narrative is, you can be sure there are many unforgettable moments that have shaped your thoughts, desires, and memories of traveling.

- During your formative years, how was travelling viewed in your family?

____

____

____

____

- What is one of the most unexpected surprises of your travelling experiences?

____

____

____

____

- Think about the people you meet when traveling. Who made the largest impact on you?

____

____

____

____

- What are some of the books or movies that have left the greatest impression on you regarding travel?

____

____

____

____

3. Practical Steps to Life-Giving Travel

If we are going to travel in a meaningful way, how will we set our priorities? Even more important than choosing the destination is determining the right fit for your abilities and personality, but also what will stretch and challenge you in new ways.

- What impact would you like to make in your globe-trotting (domestic or international)?

____

____

____

____

- What are your most important values in life?

____

____

____

____

-    How might you translate those values into a travel experience?

____

____

____

____

-    What is the next step in merging your values and your travel? (identifying service opportunities, travel broker, financial planning, etc.)

____

____

____

____

Further Resources

A Broader Definition of Travel

- *Destination Earth: A New Philosophy of Travel by a World Traveler* (Nicos Hadjicostis)
- *Travel as a Political Act* (Rick Steves)
- *The Art of Travel* (Alain de Botton)
- *Travel as Transformation* (Gregory V. Diehl)

Encouraging Stories

- *The Promise of a Pencil* (Adam Braun)
- *Wide-Open World: How Volunteering Around the Globe Changed One Family's Lives Forever* (John Marshall)
- *How to Change the World* (David Bornstein)
- *A Path Appears* (Nicholas Kristof)

Practical Steps to Life-Giving Travel

- *How to Live Your Dream of Volunteering Overseas* (Joseph Collins)
- *Volunteer: A Traveler's Guide to Making a Difference Around the World* (Lonely Planet)
- *Volunteer Vacations: Short-Term Adventures that will Benefit You and Others* (Bill McMillon)
- *Frommer's 500 Places Where You Can Make a Difference* (Andrew Mersmann)
- *Vagabonding: An Uncommon Guide to the Art on Long-Term World Travel* (Rolf Potts)

From the author…

Thanks for much for reading this book! I trust it was a help, inspiration, and provided the encouragement you needed to evaluate some things in your life. The good news is that, whatever stage we are in, we can start doing something small today to impact our future for the better.

Would you mind taking a minute to review my book on Amazon?

I certainly appreciate it!

Additional Publications by David A. Ogren

Acoustic Guitar Care 101: A Survival Guide for Beginners

GuitarQuotes: Inspiration from the World's Best Players

Market to Millions: The Ultimate Directory to Free eBook Promotion